ACKNOWLEDGEMENTS

To James and Liz Taylor Authors of

Scottish Steam Drifters

and Harvests of Herring

also South Yorkshire Television's Michael Bilton

Ronnie Summers, Chemist, Fraserburgh B.S.C.

Fraserburgh Library

Fraserburgh branch of the SPFA

Fraserburgh Herald, Editor, Alex Shand,the Herald staff,

and photographer Duncan Brown

The Royal Mission to Deep Sea Fishermen, Fraserburgh

The Macaulay Trust

DEDICATED
To the Crew of Daisy II

THE reason why I am paying a special dedication to the late crew of the Daisy II with whom I served on the fateful night at Scapa Flow, is that I am now the only one alive in the crew left to fulfil their wishes that their story should be told.

More than 800 brave men lost their lives that fateful morning of Saturday, 14th October, 1939, when the Battleship HMS Royal Oak was torpedoed and sunk in what had been thought to be an impregnable anchorage.

I never thought I would meet men of such courage in time of peril on the sea. They had great faith and that's what kept us going; our strength that night was beyond human endurance. They gave their all, and asked for nothing back.

I remember clearly, even although more than half-a-century has passed, we all worked together that night as a team, picking men out of the water, with our strength growing weaker all the time, but the Divine Spirit was with us.

Our skipper, John Gatt DSC, was a man of great faith in his God, and kept his great courage all through that night; that helped the rescue greatly - but as the long dawn came, there was a deadly silence in Scapa Flow, because over 800 men were still missing, and had no more chance of survival.

By the time dawn broke, we were now, just six men confused and tired, but amidst the sorrow that so many brave sailors had lost their lives, we had the joy of knowing that we had rescued 360 men from a watery grave.

Johnnie Duthie.

John Gatt, DSC, from Rosehearty, who was Skipper of The Daisy ll.

The crew of the Daisy ll.

John Stephen

John Gardener

Johnnie Duthie

Alex Stephen

Bobbie Duthie

HMS Royal Oak on patrol in the North Sea shortly before she was torpedoed at Scapa Flow.

Lest We Forget

(14th October 1939)

This story of that great disaster of the sinking of the Royal Oak during the Second World War was written with the grateful help of Fraserburgh author James Taylor.

This book had its beginnings in the story which I gave to the Fraserburgh Herald in 1986. A copy of that edition of the Herald found its way down to Portsmouth where many survivors came from, and when I was down at our last reunion they told me the story in the Fraserburgh Herald had finished up in the Portsmouth Guinness Book of Records.

That's when the survivors suggested that I should write a book about the disaster. I was also asked by one of our crew, the late John Stephen of Inverallochy, to record the story for posterity.

The Royal Oak survivors thought the books which had been written about the disaster seldom mentioned the heroism of the Daisy's crew, so I put a great lot of thought into it and then made up my mind to tell the story as we saw it all that night.

We in the drifter Daisy II experienced that night, the unbelievable horrors of war, and the great sorrow it brings. Some of the brave deeds done that night by both crews, Royal Oak and Daisy II, were beyond human endurance.

I have mentioned a few in my story as I look back over the years, my faith makes me believe that this madness of nations fighting against each other cannot go on forever.

We cannot fore-tell the future, but with our faith in God, we can help to make God's world a better place for all of us to live in and may the day dawn when wars shall be no more, and His peace reign over us.

'Lest we forget' is the story of a night that caused Winston Churchill to weep. Vivid memories of that horrendous incident in history are here recorded for posterity.

The might of the British Navy was enough to alarm her enemies and awaken them into early action. However the Royal Navy was precocious, but confident of security with their impregnable shield surrounding her Grand Fleet at Scapa Flow. It is therefore hard to believe that weaknesses did exist in their defences.

It was a night of heroism on 14th October 1939, and the Fraserburgh steam drifter Daisy II was right there in the centre of it.

When the terrible fight for survival was over the largest warship within British waters was to lie still and deep, however, forever present in the mind of the British nation.

Within the North-eastern anchorage of Orkney's Scapa Flow rested a floatillion of British warships, including the famous battleship HMS Royal Oak. Proudly the "Mighty Oak", as she was affectionately known, stood magnificently erect, protected by her heavy steel plated armour.

She had served with distinction on May 31, 1916, at the battle of Jutland, the largest and most impressive naval encounter ever: on that occasion her eight massive fifteen inch blazing guns wreaked devastation on the German fleet.

She was a "Royal Sovereign" class of vessel with a 31,750 ton displacement and had a top speed of twenty-one knots. To her enemies she was a fearsome sight and the legend that she carried with her into battle the resounding echo of "Drake's

Drum" forewarning victory, would have shattered any enemy morale.

However, in the still of that morning of 14th October, had they known the whole truth within that invincible vessel, many lives may well have been saved.

Little did they know that the 750 ton German submarine, the U47, had penetrated the impregnable shield at Kirk Sound on the Eastern entrance to Scapa. Once inside the Flow the Admiralty guard was down and the fleet lay at the mercy of Captain Gunther Prien and his U-boat.

He selected the largest vessel and the sleeping giant was a sitting duck as yet unaware of her fate. Ironically the German Grand Fleet was scuttled inside Scapa in 1919 following the German defeat of World War I.

However, this was not an act of revenge, but the tactful search for military targets. At 1.04 a.m. the first torpedo struck and three others followed soon after with a vengeance. The unbelievable had happened, but those on watch viewed the situation with disbelief.

Her dark mission over, Prien's U47 stealthily slipped out of the eight square miles of anchorage and through the tight Naval blockade; leaving all to darkness and the night.

It was a Naval achievement that brought fame to Captain Prien, but many years of sorrow and grief for the British people.

Standing by as tender to the Royal Oak was the Fraserburgh steam drifter Daisy II - FR 270 - and her gallant crew: John Gatt, Bobbie Duthie, John Stephen, John Gardener, Alex Stephen and Johnnie Duthie.

The Battleship had been hit with menacing accuracy both amidships and aft. Her electricity supply faltered and went

The blazing Battleship HMS Royal Oak after being mortally wounded by the torpedo salvo from U47 in Scapa Flow.

This is the final resting place of the Royal Oak at Scapa Flow.

dead, violent explosions brought catastrophic results; the vessel listed to starboard.

Luckily for the Daisy II and her crew they had moored alongside the port side of the Royal Oak and were thus clear of initial devastating explosions.

I recall that we had gone to bed, only to be wakened by a massive explosion. We went up on deck and a Naval Officer asked what was happening. Nobody seemed to know, but there was some speculation that the explosion had been made by a bomb dropped from a German aircraft which had escaped before the shore batteries could open up.

For some reason I didn't go back to bed, although the other members of the crew did. But they were to get little sleep for there was another tremendous explosion around six to eight minutes after the first one.

After the second explosion, we stood with our Skipper on deck and saw that great Battleship roll over, within six minutes of being torpedoed and all around us men were crying for help.

Just then we had to fight to save our own boat, because the mighty ship began to keel over lifting the drifter by her mooring ropes from out of the sea. The Daisy II was held by ropes from stem and bow to the larger vessel's port side.

The Daisy ll was in imminent danger of going under, and when I saw what was happening, I managed to run forward and cut the rope at the stem and immediately the drifter dropped away from the side of the Royal Oak and clear of the submerging Battleship.

For more than fifty years I have not mentioned the part I played in this because there were so many acts of bravery that

Thousands of people lined the route of the victory parade held in honour of the crew of U-47 when she returned to Germany after sinking the Royal Oak.

Crowds gathered in the streets of Berlin to welcome the crew of U-47 after she returned from sinking The Royal Oak.

The crew of U-47 were given a welcome fit for heroes at the airport when they arrived in Berlin after sinking The Royal Oak.

Adolf Hitler congratulates Lt. Gunther Prien, Commander of U-47 on his return to Germany after sinking the Royal Oak.

night and it was just something which was done because it had to be done.

There wasn't time to think. Everything happened so quickly and with little or no warning, leaving everyone in a state of shock.

Thoughts and reality were mingled with living nightmares. It was hard for us to believe what was happening around us. We were fully aware that in order to save those poor fellows from a cold icy grave, we had to leap to action stations.

Regardless of their own safety the entire crew of the Daisy ll slaved like Trojans possessed, with the willpower to pluck all of their unfortunate comrades from this turbulent, frothing pit of hell.

The task of picking survivors out of the dark, murky water became extremely more difficult. Escaping oil from the wrecked Battleship was pouring into the sea and as the twisted metal hurtled downwards to the ocean bed, this crude black mass floated continually upwards flooding the surface with a thick greasy film, thus creating havoc among the struggling survivors.

With enormous difficulty the crew of the Daisy II battled with a full scale rescue attempt. They knew there was little time, and so speed and efficiency was essential. After the final flame was swallowed up when water engulfed the last lingering piece, the night sky again plunged Scapa into a deathly darkness.

Just then our Skipper told us to light the two gaslights on our wheelhouse, so that the men swimming could see us. It was a very dark night and many of them saw us right away.

Hauling the sailors up onto the drifter became a soul-destroying job - for all were a pitiful sight, many were wounded and badly burned. It was a horrendous experience for all involved, for the mental, as well as physical torture, was to last a lifetime.

The drifter was amidst hundreds of sailors shouting for help and deliverance from their plight. One sailor who shouted to us called he could not see as the oil was in his eyes and although we tried to get hold of him he kept swimming further into the darkness crying for help. We were all overcome with grief at this point.

Then another rescued sailor with pluck and determination insisted that he re-enter the murky depths again and again to pull his shipmates clear of the deadly chemical's grasp.

A doctor serving on board HMS Royal Oak was lifted onto the Daisy II and he tirelessly treated his injured patients.

The strain must have been hard on the rescuers surrounded by such afflictions but the last call of those who were giving up the fight became a chilling experience, like the sailor who's last breath uttered: "say goodbye to my wife and children" - that is why I will never forget that dreadful night, and why none of the crew of the Daisy ll ever forgot the experiences they went through that night.

Our Skipper remained calm throughout, giving orders in a quiet controlled voice, and manoeuvring the drifter easily among the Battleship's survivors aiding the crew to bring the drowning sailors on board.

Lieutenant Benton was picked up almost immediately, but the last survivors we took aboard were a terrible sight for us all. Their skin hung in shreds down their arms. They had a lost look in their eyes and sometimes when we were pulling them up they often shouted, "don't touch me".

Some were in great pain as we struggled to help them reach safety. I remember Officer Domment as he swam towards us.

The wreath laid by the crew of The Daisy II in memory of those who lost their lives on the Royal Oak.

The War Cemetery at Longhope, Orkney, where some of the Royal Oak's crew are buried.

His body was covered with burns but desperately he yelled to us, followed by many others who saw the Daisy II's lights.

By this time it was a sea of oil and it seemed to take ages for them to   reach the safety of our deck.

Domment's charred remains of pyjamas stuck to his flesh and the rest hung in fragments; all were black with oil.

Soon the Daisy II was filling up to capacity with an assortment of survivors. Some dressed, or in pyjamas, but most half naked and suffering terrible scars of warfare.

The crew of the Daisy ll threw anything that could float into the sea in the hope that survivors could cling to until they were rescued.

This proved to be a blessing to those who were unable to reach the rescuing craft in time. The intense cold presented the strongest swimmers with problems and they were glad of anything to support them while they waited.

I remember that the pieces of wood we cast into the sea saved a few lives. Cadet Owen and a young marine clung to the same piece of wood till we rescued them. Most of the men towards the end of our rescue had to be hauled out of the water as they were too weak.

I'll always remember one poor chap called Finlay who came alongside. He had just lost his friend who disappeared below the surface and he was resigned to go under too, until he saw the Daisy's light.

Finlay was almost gone, but we picked him up and laid him on Skipper Gatt's bed, as he was in a bad way.

We had to be granted strength from God as I fail to believe it was done on our own! We were wearied with the continued strain of toil and unnerving experiences of so many badly wounded and dying men thrust upon all by the horror of modern war. Its evil capabilities had just reached home with a vengeance.

The Biblical quote: "Be still and know that I am God" rang in our ears and this gave us great strength.

Teardrops fell throughout the long night's search as the Daisy II's crew lowered their ears to hear faint calls of the lost to be rescued. "Don't leave us Daisy" came some painful cries of suffering sailors with wounds beyond endurance. These were to be the last, for the sea claimed the rest.

Hearts of Oak it could be said as they were all brave men: those who were sacrificed by war to a watery grave, and those who survived the "Mighty Oak's" demise.

But still further was the heroism displayed by the crew of Fraserburgh's Daisy II as it was they who pulled to safety 360 members of the Royal Oak's crew from the freezing oily waters of Scapa Flow that fateful October night.

The grimness of the situation fell on the British people with devastating results as this was a moment in history few would ever forget. Winston Churchill had warned the Navy to strengthen their defence and when he was first told by his secretary of the disaster and the death of 833 sailors, tears flooded his eyes as he said: "Those poor men in the icy cold waters of Scapa Flow."

I would like to thank James Taylor for his time he has given to me in the writing of the book; I am very grateful to him. The story is a true reflection of what happened that night in the icy waters of Scapa Flow. Our crew was all there that night; now I am the only one left to fulfil their wishes in this story of the Royal Oak disaster; the story about the brave crew of the Fraserburgh drifter Daisy ll, and Skipper John Gatt.

This floral tribute in the shape of an anchor was laid by Royal Oak survivor Bob Hayhoe.

Former crewman on U-47 Ernst Deiallas, laid this wreath at the memorial on Southsea Common, Portsmouth.

I have said this before and I will say it again. Books and papers have written about this sad story but many questions have been left unanswered. We as a crew were never asked any questions, so it has been a long silence for us over the years, but we saw it all from the beginning to the end, and I will say again it was a night for heroism; also a night for sorrow.

I have only mentioned some of the brave deeds done that night by both crews, especially the Royal Oak's crew. They were the cream of the British Navy, with an average age of 30 years. As they held on to the bits of wood they found floating, they sang, they joked and many died.

Some wanted to leave the Daisy II and help their pals in the water, others held on to their shipmates as they became weaker in the water.

Rear Admiral HEC Blagrove refused a lifebuoy that was offered to him, and he spent the last few minutes of his life helping others. I will never forget the bravery also of our crew that night, and when I think about them, I always recall these words:

When day is done a person turns and says a last goodbye although we cannot understand where they must go or why but as they leave our tears and sorrows behind they move ahead to seek a place that every soul must find.

The sinking of the Royal Oak, commanded by Rear Admiral Blagrove was one of the biggest disasters of Second World War.

Our whole nation was shocked when they heard the news. We were always made believe that Scapa Flow was impregnable, and the safest Naval Base in the world. How wrong they were that night. It became a nightmare to the crews of both ships.

The Royal Oak was a floating furnace within minutes of being hit by the last two torpedoes. She was just back from a

Laying wreaths at the memorial to the Royal Oak dead at Southsea Common, Portsmouth. From left are Johnnie Duthie, Herbert Herrman, Ernst Deiallas and Bob Hayhoe.

patrol in the North Sea, where it was blowing gale force winds, so the crew were all tired and went to bed early, feeling very safe inside Scapa Flow, but that was not to be.

Commander Prien and his crew and submarine U47 manoeuvred, with great skill, through an almost impossible space at Kirk Sound. It took great navigational skill to get into Scapa Flow. She slowly crept up near the Royal Oak, firing one torpedo, then minutes later she fired another two torpedoes, which finished the great Battleship. Sadly the Oak's crew never had a chance to fight back. After the last salvo of torpedoes hit her, she began to turn over.

It was hard for us to believe that this was the last time we would see the Royal Oak, and many of her crew we knew so well as we started taking survivors aboard. The Oak was a big cloud of smoke, and men running all over the ship trying to find out what had happened. The Admiral and the Captain were as much confused as the crew. We saw the sadness of it all, and it is still with us over the years. That's why I named the book Lest We Forget.

Our crew on the Daisy II were all fishermen and we knew how dangerous the sea could be, not only in War but also in the great storms in peacetime, but this situation was different.

We had only six of a crew on the Daisy II and we knew it was going to be a long sad night for us, as hundreds of people were in the water crying to be saved, so with the faith we had we found strength to carry on.

We had forgotten the time of day, we only knew when dawn came. The darkness disappeared and we were thankful for that to help us in the rescue, as we took them aboard the Daisy they all asked the same question, 'Have you my pal aboard, his name is so and so?' We could not remember all their names. They were a grand lot of seamen, typical of the British Navy. Some of our survivors were back to the War again, after a few weeks' leave.

A sad moment as dead shipmates are remembered - William Shearer from Thurso, Johnnie Duthie, Inverallochy, and Philip Whyte, meet at a reunion held at Southsea Common, Portsmouth.

Stan Cole one of the survivors of the Royal Oak came with his wife all the way from South Wales to see us in Fraserburgh. It was one of the greatest moments of my life when the door bell rang and here was one of the Oak's survivors.

I tried not to cry and so did he, but that was impossible. He never said he was coming on to see us because he wanted to give us a surprise, so we had a great reunion together. I thought it was a great gesture coming all these miles from South Wales to see us.

One of the cooks of the Iron Duke missed his picket boat from Kirkwall pier, so he came with us on Daisy and was going to stay the night on board Royal Oak, but he did not get back in the morning to his own ship the Iron Duke. The poor fellow went down with the Royal Oak and was lost.

Taffy Davis, who was in the military band, said that it was like going down a steep cliff as the battleship rolled at 50°. He stepped on to the Royal Oak's slippery blister on her side, and was hauled aboard our drifter.

L H Tunnicliff said: "I rolled on to my back to rest for a while, as I was full of oil, then I remembered nothing more till I was taken aboard a boat which he found out later was the Daisy II."

Our skipper John Gatt did a heroic job in the wheelhouse taking our ship alongside the men in the water as they swam for their lives, so it made it easier for us to get hold of them. Some became to weak to swim, many disappeared before our eyes with no strength left to keep afloat.

Another great part of heroism was done by our engineer who stood by the engine below, while we had 50° of a list and being pulled over by the Royal Oak to the starboard side.

Our bow rope was too tight to let go, so we had to cut our bow rope to get clear, and our ship slid down the Royal Oak's port side. That's when we began to leak, and all that time our

26

A personal tribute to dead shipmates...Johnnie Duthie lays a wreath at the memorial on Southsea Common, Portsmouth.

engineer stood by the engine below. Our leak did not get any bigger, so we carried on picking up survivors, in all 360 men but sadly 833 went down with her.

We often paid a visit to the Royal Oak's crew. The night she was torpedoed we were only 1 1/2 hours back on our drifter.

Churchill in his tears had still a word for Commander Prien of U47. He said it was a great navigational feat. Prien was later lost in the Atlantic on patrol.

Royal Oak survivors with the Shearers at Thurso staying for the night on their way home on leave.

I will say to the younger generation: this was the price paid for the great freedom we hold dear; let's not forget it. As we took the last man aboard, we were all greatly touched with deep emotion, as we had to leave most of the crew behind. Never in our lives had we felt such terrible sadness, most of them were trapped inside the Royal Oak, and right up until today, that spot has been kept as their war grave. If the politicians of all nations had seen this disaster at Scapa Flow that night, war would be in their last thoughts I will say to the parents and friends who lost their loved ones that night

They grow not old as we that are left grow old
Age shall not weary them nor the years condemn
At the going down of the sun and in the morning
We shall remember them.

Former enemies united in the same tragedy...former Royal Oak sailor, Welshman Taffy Davies and Herbert Herman, former crewman on the U-47 meet at a reunion in Portsmouth.

Johnny Duthie with George Clelands, from South Shields, at a survivors' reunion. George, aged 86 when this picture was taken, is the oldest survivor of the disaster.

Some of the Royal Oak survivors with friends during a reunion at Portsmouth.

Johnnie Duthie, the last surviving member of the crew of the Daisy ll welcomes Royal Oak survivor Stan Cole, from Wales, to his home in Fraserburgh.

Survivors and their wives gather to lay wreaths at the memorial to the Royal Oak dead on Southsea Common, Portsmouth.

Johnnie Duthie and his wife Isabella, at a reunion in Portsmouth for the suvivors of the Royal Oak.

Harold Wernam, Johnnie Duthie and Reg Bendall attending a reunion for the suvivors of the Royal Oak disaster at Portsmouth.